Dashleigh the Dachshund

Eva Bea Knight

Dashleigh the Dachshund

by Eva Bea Knight

ISBN: 978-1-0686118-8-9

A CIP catalogue record for this book is available
from the British Library.

For more information about other books and upcoming titles go to:

facebook.com/EvaBeaKnightBooks   instagram.com/evabeaknight.author

Dashleigh
the Dachshund

written and illustrated
by Eva Bea Knight

Dashleigh is our dachshund.
He has a glossy black coat with
caramel-coloured patches on his fur.
His chubby chin is as brown as gravy.

Dashleigh's awesome ears do various tricks.

And he shows all his TRUE feelings!

We're not sure about Dashleigh. Is he more adorable than annoying?

Or is he more annoying than adorable?

We are so happy that Dashleigh is just the right size to carry.

We are so miserable when Dashleigh's snores keep us awake at night.
SNORT
ZZZZZZ
RATTLE
HONK-SHOO

We giggle when Dashleigh welcomes us home like we've been away for a whole year! Even if it's only been five minutes.

We are confused when Dashleigh glares hungrily at his empty food bowl JUST AFTER he's eaten a **HUGE** dinner!

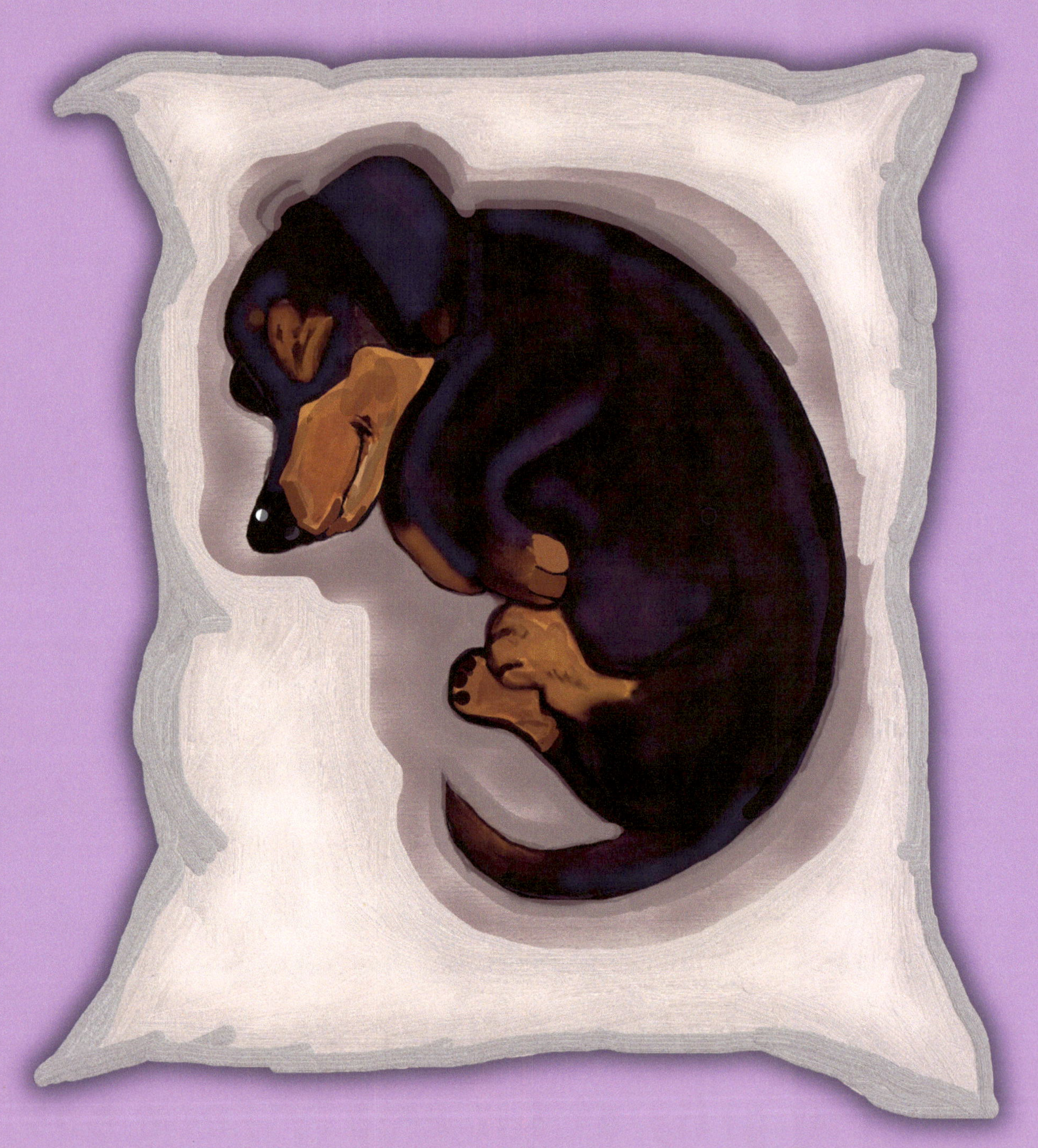

We find it so CUTE when Dashleigh curls up in the shape of a croissant on his favourite cushion.

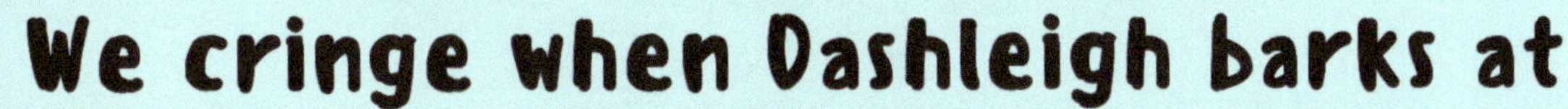

We cringe when Dashleigh barks at
ALL cats...
and at dogs that are...
TOO BIG
too small
exactly the same size
and at other animals that move.

When we are stuck in bed
feeling poorly, we appreciate
Dashleigh keeping us company.

We apologise to
Dashleigh whenever
we use the vacuum
cleaner.

We're not sure
why he growls
and grumbles
at it.

We don't worry about missing the doorbell. No-one gets inside without Dashleigh's permission.
WOOF!
GRRRR!
RUFF!